# Building of a Champion

## Determination ▪ Desire ▪ Dedication

*How I Became a Champion in Life!*

## THE AVIS BROWN-RILEY STORY

PAGE PUBLISHING, INC.
New York, NY

First originally published by Page Publishing, Inc. 2017

ISBN 978-1-64138-342-4 (Paperback)
ISBN 978-1-64138-343-1 (Digital)

Printed in the United States of America

Avis Brown is not only an icon, but she is what young girls of color like my daughters strive to be and look up to. She not only stands as a role model for girls of color but all girls alike. I have had the honor and privilege of knowing Avis for a few years now, and her life's accomplishments and story are something we can all stand in awe of. As a former NBA basketball player and current member of the Texas judiciary, I can honestly say it is stories like Avis' that make this great country what it is today.

Judge Joe Stephens

I have had the great privilege and honor to know Avis Brown and the Gordon Brown family throughout my years in San Diego and Southern California and the huge impact the Brown Family had, and has, on the game of golf in the major region. Avis carries on with the high passion and love for the game and sport of golf and brings those characteristics to everyone she encounters in the game and for the good of the game. Avis is truly a champion and spends her life building champions around her.

Tom Addis III, PGA
Executive Director/CEO
Past President, PGA of America
Southern California PGA

We are constantly looking for positive role models and those individuals who we can call Champions in Life. My friend Avis Brown is one of those inspiring individuals. As a champion golfer, she suddenly found herself facing her toughest round of golf ever, when she was faced with a life and death situation of battling breast cancer. To no one's surprise, she broke par and survived Breast Cancer. Avis shares her amazing journey of courage and her walk in life with the world through her life story.

She is an African American woman golf trail blazer, but more importantly- she is a woman golf trail blazer who has blazed the trail for the next generation of young women golfers.

Renee Powell
Clearview Golf Club
Lifetime LPGA Tour Member and
Class A PGA of America Member

When I reflect back on our friendship which spans 30 plus years...the words I'd use to best describe Avis Brown-Riley are strength, resolve and courage!

Willie Ervin Toney, Jr.
PGA Assistant Head Golf Professional
The Olympic Club

Kissi Couture, Makenna and Morgan Rodriguez with gratitude and love endorse our friend and benevolent humanitarian, Avis Brown. Avis is on a mission endeavoring to make a global footprint for positive world change. She enlightens and educates, making mankind aware of all the positive contributions contributed by all ethnicities. She is an avid golfer and has offered a plethora of services to the golf community, sparking a fire of enthusiasm for minority girls in the golf arena. Avis is our Shero.

Makenna & Morgan Rodriguez of Kissi Couture

# Contents

For generations, our society has placed tremendous emphasis on *winning* and *losing*, so much so that we often forget to celebrate the valuable life experiences that are gained.

There is no substitute for life experiences, and we can all benefit from gaining knowledge, getting opportunities, and being empowered with everyday life experiences. Whether a schoolteacher, store clerk, housewife, CEO, watching a baby take their first steps, trying to succeed in the classroom, or climbing the ladder in corporate America, the knowledge and opportunities one gains from everyday life activities and events contribute toward our spiritual growth, help to build the readiness level to face and conquer daily challenges, and allow us to achieve our dreams.

I believe that one of the greatest gifts a person can give to another is the sharing of life experiences. As our forefathers have proven, through this gift, we help to build character, hope, and a road map for self-defined success.

This book is for anyone who dreams the dream of winning in life and seeing how the three Ds (dedication, desire, and determination) can empower you to reach the interpersonal rewards that life has to offer.

I dedicate this book to our Heavenly Father and his Son, who is my Lord and Savior and my rock. He has blessed me with two wonderful parents; their love, support, and personal sacrifices have allowed me to reach beyond the stars.

To my husband and soul mate, James Riley, you have bought joy to my heart and added years to life. To my children, family, and friends, thanks for all your support.

A special thanks to the Avis Brown-Riley Golf Extravaganza team. Your courage, spirit, and leap of faith drive us, and because of you, we are able to move mountains and help empower others.

Finally, to Gordon Brown Jr., my mentor, my brother and best friend, thank you for your unconditional love, support, and guidance.

> Above all else, guard your affections. For they influence everything else in your life.
>
> —Proverbs 4:23
> Taken from the Living Bible

# Chapter One

# Competition Is a Part of Everyday Life

## 1. Learning to Compete

We begin to learn how to compete from the time we are born. A toddler cries when they want to compete for their parents' attention, siblings compete to gain the love and affection of their parents. We compete in academics, sports, and on the job. Competition is a part of everyday life, and society places tremendous emphasis centered on winning and losing.

Dr. Thomas M. Brunner is a licensed clinical psychologist who specializes in advanced assessment and treatment of children, adolescents, and adults, and notes the following:

> "As a child counselor and parent, I have experienced and witnessed the deep craving parents feel to see their children triumph in the competitive arena. Whether academic or athletic, there is a fire in the belly when it comes to competing. In my counseling work with gifted students, youth athletes and highly competitive families, I have discovered something far more important than the win/loss record. Something more golden than the Gold Medal. A character mettle forged much stronger than trophy metal. Something that you as a parent (or competitor) should heed if you want your child to compete in the fullest rather

than in the most primitive sense in the arena of life.

What do I mean by the most primitive sense? "Too many youth athletes get over focused on getting the win," says Dr. Scott Goldman, PhD, a colleague of mine and fellow father. He is also Director of Clinical and Sports Psychology at the University of Arizona, and counsels college athletes. He says, "I tell our athletes all the time, if you just want to win, go play against a 4th grader. But if you want your win to have meaning, play against someone who can beat you". I would add this: you learn and grow much more from loses than wins."

"The losses build your resilience, your adaptability. Your ability to get up after being kicked in the stomach, literally or metaphorically. Scott then made a critical point for all you parents to chew on: if the focus is on child development, the competitive event is only one component. The other component is who is helping your child understand (and stand back from) their experience of the event. He said a common experience is college athletes telling stories of how if they won the game, they got ice cream, and if they lost, they went straight home. Thus, winning becomes bound up with acceptance and losing means one is not accepted or loved.

"But winning IS IMPORTANT," you say, adding, "Spare us the mushy ice cream stories and tell us how to make our kid the next star of the team." Hey, I feel the heat. I have given inspirational talks to my 7-year-old William on how important it is to compete heartily. I am a serious competitor. Why? Because I feel just like my friend and fellow competitive cyclist Matt Blair, a father of two young children.

He said: "Being competitive is a requirement to survive and be successful. In order to succeed, we must embrace our competitive nature, challenge ourselves, and overcome the obstacles that keep us from our dreams."

He then went into Old Wise Man mode and tapped into the core of my blog when he said: "As a child, being competitive can help children develop the necessary life tools that are most important for a successful life." Matt's focus on the bigger picture, on the importance of your child learning "life tools", hits the bull's eye. So why do so many coaches, parents, and children over focus on the primitive target of winning and losing the next game and lose focus on the bigger and more noble target of building tools that will serve them as they struggle the ups and downs of marriage, career challenges, loss, and maybe even trauma.

In short, the tools that will serve them till death. I have several hypotheses about what drives the narrow focus on winning. We have evolved over millions of years to want to equate winning with survival. To believe there is a winner and a loser. Who wins? The competing tribe or our tribe? Do we kill the predator or does it kill us?

Dozens of psychological experiments prove that when people are put into circumstances where they must compete, raw and primitive energy is unleashed. The beast within is awakened. It's us against them. And that is why millions tune in to sports every weekend, we crave to witness the raw grandeur of blood, sweat, and tears being shed for the glory of being the last one standing. Are we that far from the Roman Coliseum?

We also relish the idea of the underdog coming out on top, taking what was not theirs and may not have even seemed within their reach. An epic example being the U.S. Olympic Hockey team upsetting the Russians in the 1980 Winter Olympics in Lake Placid. No one thought this was possible. One final hypothesis is that for some people winning IS the end all be all. I quote Vince Lombardi, one of the winningest NFL coaches of all time: "Winning isn't everything . . . it is the only thing". But winning at what? Beating who?

## The Trap of Relative Success and Why Competing With Yourself is Best

I argue that the greatest competition is within oneself, and you should be most focused on beating yourself. The enemy is within. In other words, the best athletes even after a win are asking themselves what they did wrong. Sloppy wins are no better than bad losses. The focus should not be on whether your child won, but on whether they used their set of physical and mental tools to hit their "sweet spot," their potential that day.

If the focus is more on what unique skill sets they bring to the game, and you or coach works with them on rigorously developing these skills, then they will not over focus on beating someone else, but on expanding their potential. My friend and fellow father John Lee served up a great example of this when he reminded me about what he calls the competition and the "trap relative success." I quote him fully: "In the dark

days of Apple computers they were focused fool-
ishly on competing with Microsoft, in the PC
market. They wasted their resources in a game
that promised only relative success and delivered
concrete failure.

Upon his return, Steve Jobs withdrew Apple
from this competition and set about to excel in
a different field. The wisdom in that is, do what
YOU do well. Don't let your competitors define
success. Help teach your children as early as possible to find their center.

Help them strive to excel in their productive
use to others. If we let Nike define competition
to our children we fail."

Now, let your child also know that what
Matt Blair says something to take to Heart: "If
you have given your best, pushed yourself as hard
as possible and you still don't win, rejoice in your
effort. Rejoice." Sometimes you want to celebrate
even defeats, when they played to their potential.

**The End Goal**

The end goal of competition is to accelerate the development of the tools you or your
child need to reliably hit the performance sweet
spot on any given day. The focus must be on the
development of tools that will serve anyone when
they are called upon to exhibit character and/or
leadership throughout their life . . . not on wins
and losses. Though wins and losses must be part
of the journey.

See more of Dr. Thomas M. Brunner's work at http://www.doc-
torbrunner.com/teach-your-child-to-be-competitive-to-ready-them-
for-the-arena-of-life/#sthash.29zHNuqm.dpuf.

15

## 2. Building Blocks

I have two amazing parents. They had four children, all playing junior golf at the same time. Talk about your sibling rivalry! My brother Horace was the first African American to win the San Diego County Junior Golf Association Junior Golfer of the Year, and Horace and Oran both won CIF High School Golf Championships.

We each had the three Ds (desire, dedication, or determination) to become the best, and the competition was extremely fierce. I believed that we infused passion for the game with zealous and fierce competition among ourselves.

In fact, my two brothers, Gordon Jr. and Horace, built two golf holes in the canyon behind our house, and when we could not get to the golf course, we would spend hours playing the Masters and US Open. Later, my father built us a small putting green and purchased a hitting net to further hone our skills.

During the summer months, our mother would pack us a lunch and drive us to a little PAR 3 course. Looking back, being the only girl and playing against my older brothers definitely helped me to build the mental toughness needed to compete and become successful.

**Foundations are the basis upon which
something stands or is supported.**

The GAME      The Rules      The Approach

Imagine the challenge of having three junior golf champions, all with diverse and unique personalities. Fortunately for us, my parents focus was on the development of tools that helped us to exhibit strong moral character, humility, and celebrating the love for the game and life and not on wins and losses. The building blocks they taught us were the importance of the game, the approach, and the rules.

## The Game

The game of golf consists of more than getting the ball in the hole in the least amount of stokes. We were taught that the game was more than having a good swing, shooting the course record, or winning junior tournaments; it encompasses much more.

## The Approach

Golf is just a game; you should build your life around golf and not golf around your life, and the intrinsic attributes associated with golf help define you as a person.

## The Rules

The rules in sports and life have a basic purpose; they are in place to test your skills, mind, body, and soul and used as a measurement to establish a baseline of performance. They are not to be broken.

Little did I realize that these tools would serve me well, as I struggled with the ups and downs of college, playing on the mini tours, selecting a career, and even trauma.

# Chapter Two

# Golf Is a Metaphor for Life

Some parents push, encourage, and sometimes can be overbearing, a little obnoxious, but these things are in an attempt to give their child the best advantage they can before it's time for them to solely embark on the journey called life.

They lie awake, pondering on their approach to effectively communicate ways to handle different situations that their child may face on a day-to-day basis. They seek opportunities to pull their child aside, to sit down with them and explain the many ways to have a good life. They beat dead horses, just to come to the conclusion that their child will learn how to carry themselves in a respectful manner, learn how to manage time, be sociable, likeable, and ultimately learn how to win in the game of life.

Parents have been there and done that and truly understand what the game of life can do for us all.

Whether it is learning how to control one's emotions or receiving an invite to play softball, tennis, or golf with the boss, there are some things the child will just have to trust them on!

So the parents sign them up for PGA Junior League without their discretion. They yearn for an inkling that golf could possibly come before the Xbox, Playstation4, or sleepover. For the more serious kids, parents decide it's time; they will sign up for Junior Golf Academy to get that one-on-one attention from Ricky, Jane, and K.J.

Not holding their breath, waiting for that thank you that tends to come a lot later down the road. To make them feel better about all they have just endured, parents allow them to head into the Professional Shop to see Lauren, Adidas, or Nike so they can buy the newest trinket, the hottest driver, or nicest jacket on the rack. You see, getting your child involved in golf has its benefits in the long run, much like placing money away toward a retirement fund. The earlier you start, the more rewarding it can prove to be down the line. All of which supports the economy in more ways than one has time to describe! Get involved sooner than later. Prepare your kids for life through experiencing a game that is no better representative for building life skills and memorable experiences.

There is no such thing as failure, unless
you accept that as the end result!
Tee it high, and let it fly!

## 1. My Early Golf Experience

Once you catch the golf fever, golf becomes more than a game; it becomes a way of life. I started playing golf at age seven and as far back as I can remember; I often found myself dreaming at night and daydreaming in school about hitting that cutch shot and making a ten-foot putt to win the tournament. In sharing my golf and life experiences with you, please remember that "Golf is just a game and the intrinsic attributes associated with it, helps to build character, it does not define who you are."

As a young junior golfer, I rarely looked at the trees lining the fairways. I did not hit it far enough to worry about the bunkers until my third shot, in order to make a par, I developed a superior short game which contributed to my early success. At age ten, I won the prestigious Optimist Junior World Tournament held annually since 1968 in San Diego, California.

By the time I was fifteen, my long game had caught to my short game, and tree lines became a little more visible, the bunkers seem bigger, and finally my superb short game allowed me to challenge any golf hole with confidence.

As a high school golfer, I was among the best in the county. Winning golf championships left and right and representing the San Diego County Junior Golf Association on several winning teams.

Champions are not born, and there is no secret formula for building a champion. However, foundations are the basis upon which something stands or is supported. Yes! My parents had been there, done that. They used their life experiences, provided me with a solid foundation, and instilled three components that allowed me to be very competitive and achieve early success.

Also, another key factor, I learned to play for myself, learned to love the game for me, and understood at an early age the importance of the game, the approach, and the rules. Little did I know that my ability to integrate these three components into my daily life experiences would one day help to save my life.

## 2. The Game

The game of golf consists of more than getting the ball in the hole in the least amount of stokes. I learned that the game was more than having a good swing, shooting the course record, or winning forty-six junior tournaments; it encompasses much more.

The game provides an opportunity to develop mental toughness and builds character. It requires self-discipline, it teaches you perseverance, integrity, and courtesy, and because it is an individual sport, when on the golf course, you learn to depend on your wits, make sound decisions, and live and accept the consequences of your actions.

The other interpersonal skills inherent to golf are learning to be responsible, developing self-confidence, learning good time management skills, and applying these skills during your everyday life, in addition to learning how to socially interact with people from all lifestyles. Finally and most importantly, it teaches you humility.

Regardless of your athletic ability, you will never be able to master the game. However, regardless of your skill level or golf aspirations, you can achieve a level of personal enjoyment or gratification in its attainment by showing ardent love and affection for the game.

My father, who has been playing golf for more than sixty years and yet to master the game, still has the same gleam in eyes and sparkle in his voice each time he plays or gives a lesson. He truly has an ardent love and affection for the game and sharing this love with anyone who will listen.

## 3. The Approach

For the purpose of this conversation, Webster defines *approach* as "in order to create a desired result; an example would be; hitting the golf shot from the fairway to the green."

You have a one-stroke lead; you are in the final group and need a birdie to set the course record, but a par will clinch the tournament. You are one hundred yards out and have your favorite and trusty wedge in your hands. The pin is tucked in the right corner of the green, and there is water five yards behind the green. Do you go for the pin or go for the center of the green?

This exercise is not designed to test your level of commitment, desire, dedication, or determination but to show you that golf is a game and, like everyday events in your life, is filled with having to make tough decisions. How you approach your decisions are based on whether or not you want to take a course of action that will lead to a positive desired result.

This has always been my approach to the game. Golf teaches strategy; how do I manage (navigate) the ball around the course? Do I play aggressive on the par fives and play conservative on the par threes? When and where do I gamble or take the miracle shot? I learned that the best golfers were thinkers; they had a game plan for a particular course and stuck to it. Using this approach ultimately made the round much more enjoyable and allowed me to shot the best score possible."

As a junior golfer, golf was a business for me. I set long- and short-term goals. I learned how to manage my time, set schedules, practiced more than I played. I entered each tournament with the belief that I was going to win. More importantly, I learned at an early age that golf is much more enjoyable if you make it fun.

I also took time off from golf and enjoyed just being a kid, a teenager, and a young adult. In my professional career, I came to realize that you cannot relive each eighteen holes of golf or tournament. I placed a lot of emphasis on the following: Golf is just a game; you should build your life around golf and not golf around your life, and the intrinsic attributes associated with golf helps to define you as a person.

Finally, from my many life experiences, I have witnessed that early golf success is not a prelude for future success, and a lack of that early golf success does not prohibit future success.

## The E-Generation Approach

I am amazed at the low scores and skills of the previous generation of golfers. Can you image what Arnold Palmer, Jack Nicholas, Nancy Lopez, Byron Nelson, Lee Trevino, and Ben Hogan would shoot if they had the technology used today.

Yes! The technological advances in golf equipment and golf balls make a difference. Thirty years later, I now hit the driver twenty yards farther with the same swing I used in my twenties.

Here are six advantages:

1. High-tech golf equipment
2. Information highway (Internet)
3. GPS tracking
4. Specialized training and fitness equipment
5. Sports psychologist and trainers
6. Digital training tools to improve the golf swing, including driving ranges

There is no argument that today's golf equipment is far superior; everything from golf clubs, golf balls, and golf shoes, all designed to enhance performance. The Internet has provided the E-generation golfer with access to digital online golf swing analysis, golf information to include easy access to research golf's past, present, and future.

GPS tracking has taken the guesswork out of getting the correct yardage. The specialized training, equipment, tools, and support team allows the professional golfer to focus on one thing, playing golf at their peak performance day in and day out.

As we have witnessed, with these advantages, the majority of E-generation golfers (junior and college golfers) are easily outperforming their old-school competitor's scores, the mythical 59 for eighteen holes is a thing of the past, and tournament 72 hole scores are falling left and right.

With the emergence of technological advances, one would assume that the E-generation golfers have advantages when it comes to the approach.

However, this is not the case. The E-generation's approach to the game has become more complex. They must incorporate the new technology, be able to process a tremendous amount of information along with learning how to compete on the golf course. Bigger, faster, and stronger does not always equate to better.

The successful E-generation golfer still has to learn how to think their way around the golf course, use a golf course game plan, practice more than they play, learn how to make critical decisions at the right time, and finally, remember that golf is just a game. Regardless of their athletic ability, they will never be able to master the game.

Regardless of your skill level or golf aspirations, you can achieve a level of personal enjoyment or gratification in its attainment by showing ardent love and affection for the game.

Your approach to the game of golf dictates your enjoyment of the game, and how you apply the three Ds (desire, dedication, or determination) plays a critical factor in becoming a champion in life. If you think about it, the game and your approach to the game is governed by rules.

## 4.  *The Rules*

For the purpose of this conversation, Webster defines *rule* as "a prescribe guide for conduct or action; a standard of judgment; an accept procedure, custom or habit."

From early childhood, we apply rules bestowed on us. They are guidelines that help society maintain order, conduct, and actions. Established rules help to keep the playing field level, to protect us from those who seek to take advantage in order to get ahead.

Rules are meant to be broken—*not*.

This belief has permeated throughout history, and it applies to all facets of life. You are expected not to cheat on your income taxes, not drive the highways without a motor vehicle registration or driver licenses, but there are those who do. If you break rules and get away with it, without anyone knowing about it, what is really achieved?

The rules in sports have a basic purpose; they are in place to test your skills, mind, body, and soul and used as a measurement to establish a baseline of performance.

The rules of golf help to maintain our game's proud traditions and rich heritage and help to govern play, equipment, and etiquette. Although you will never be able to master the game, you can master the rules of the game.

There are two special rules that have stuck with me throughout the years:

1.  I have never met a good golfer who has broken a rule and not called the violation on himself or herself. No matter how great or small the stake or prize, no rule violation is worth a person's integrity.

2.  There are no rules that limit a person from playing and enjoying the wonderful game of golf. Here is one of my favorite golf quotes:

The hardest shot is a mashie at 90 yards from the green where the ball has to be played against an oak tree, bounced back into the sand trap, hits a stone, bounce on the green, and rolls into the cup. That shot is so difficult, I have only made it once.

—Zeppo Mark, *The Love of Golf*

As any golfer knows, the rules are an inherent part of you, a habit. Following the rules becomes more than a matter of pride; it is the omnipotent part of the game that you dare not test or break. As put by one of the game's greats:

You might as well praise a man for robbing a bank as to praise him for playing by the rules.

—Bobby Jones, *The Love of Golf*

The next time someone in your foursome starts to pick a pebble from behind their ball while in a hazard, kindly remind that it is a two-stroke penalty and watch the express on their face.

Rules may be broken everywhere else, but not in *golf.* I strongly recommend that before you tee it again, study the USGA Rules of Golf, which can be located in your local pro shop, golf shop, or on the Internet.

If you think about it, a sport is just like life. You have to learn and try to master the game, have an approach (game plan), and know the rules. *Golf really is a metaphor for life.*

# Chapter Three

# My Junior Golf Career

My amazing journey began in San Diego, California. I am the second-youngest of five siblings, born to Gordon Sr. and Harriet Brown. My father introduced me to the game of golf at age seven, but it was my mother that took my three brothers and me back and forth to the golf course and tournaments. Our hardworking, humble, and devoted parents' sacrifices paid off.

I won my first junior golf tournament at the age of eight. At the age of ten, I became the first African American to win the prestigious Junior World Golf Championship. I learned to celebrate my three other Junior World Golf Championship trophies. Each trophy meant that I was among the best girls junior golfer in the world.

My hard work, along with the three Ds, really paid off. During a nine-year span, as a member of the San Diego Junior Golf Association, I won forty-six golf tournaments and was awarded as the number one Girl Junior Golfer five times.

While in the 10 and under, 11–12, and 13–14 divisions, winning became second nature. As a fifteen-year-old, I quickly realized that there was tremendous competition in the 15–17 division, and winning was not easy.

By the end of the summer, I finally started to believe that I had what it took to compete with San Diego's top female golfers. I had finished second in the San Diego Evening Tribute tournament to San Diego's notable top female golfer, Sharon Barrett. This was definitely the turning point in my young golf career.

By my final campaign year in the 15–17 division, my hard work, combined with the three Ds, previous golf and life experiences, and maturity, kicked in. I had a year of exciting and fun golf experiences that people dream of and movies are made for.

Here are just a few of the highlights:

- I was the number one player on the Samuel J. Morse High School Boys Golf team.
- I was invited to play in the Andy Williams San Diego Pro-Am with United States Open Champion Jerry Pate. I had an opportunity to meet the legendary actor Scat Man Cruthers (*Lady Sings the Blues* and *The Shining*), and from a short distance, I saw Bob Hope and President Gerald Ford.
- I played on the victorious San Diego team in the Junior Girls America Cup.
- I won the prestigious Marvin K. Brown San Diego County Match Play Championship.
- I won the prestigious San Diego Evening Tribute Championship
- I won the Southern California girls qualifying for the national PGA Junior.

- I amazingly won ten of sixteen San Diego Junior Golf Association events, finished second twice, and third three times.

## *Foundations Are the Basis upon which Something Stands or Is Supported*

Champions are not born, and there is no secret formula for building of a champion. However, foundations are the basis upon which something stands or is supported. Yes! My parents had been there, done that. They used their life experiences, provided me with a solid foundation, and instilled in me three components that allowed me to be very competitive and achieve early success.

Thanks, Mom and Dad!

## *The Game, the Approach, and the Rules*

A seven-year-old from Southeast San Diego began an amazing journey. During a ten-year span, she took on the social challenges, overcame barriers, and made personal sacrifices and amassed one of the best junior golf accomplishments in San Diego's history. Let's sees where the journey takes her next.

# Chapter Four

# My College Golf Career

If you thought I had a great junior golf career, well, my college years took my breath away, and I came in with a bang. Immediately after my high school graduation, I decided to play in the San Diego Women's City Amateur Golf Championship. To my knowledge, no other African American female had ever played in this event.

Even though it was just another tournament for me, I felt the butterflies. I guess I realized that this was the next step in the pursuit of my dream—playing on the LPGA. For our non-golfers, this shift is like moving from VP of Products to COO. I had always taken the approach that if my game was sharp, I could win any tournament. My practice sessions were not going well, my nerves were shot, and my anxiety level was high.

Finally, I broke down and asked my oldest brother, Gordon Jr., who had always had a calming effect on me, if he would caddy for me. He knew my game and the three courses we were going to play, Balboa Park, Torrey Pines North and South, inside out.

The first round was at Balboa Park, and we were very confident. We did not know it then, but looking back, Gordon and I actually put the game, the approach, and the rules in practice.

The first nine holes was a disaster; I shot a 41 but came back with a 36 on the back nine, for a score of 77. The second round was at Torrey Pines North, and once again, we arrived at the first tee very confident. You guessed it; I shot a 41 on the first nine holes but came back with a 37 on the back nine, for a score of 78.

After thirty-six holes, I was tied with Patti Berendt, who just happened to have played on my high school golf team. Having played with Patti for two years, I knew that she wanted this championship more than anything. The final round was set for Torrey Pines South.

I had managed to fight off my inner demons and was even par for fifteen holes.

I held a three-stokes lead with three holes to play.

Going to the last hole, I had a one-stroke lead. Patti had already hit her third shot to the Par 5 and was on the putting green. Gordon Jr. handed me the right club to hit to the green. It was the first time in three rounds that I did not listen to him. I selected the club I wanted to hit.

At the end of the round, Patti and I were tied. On the way to the scorer's tent, Gordon Jr. said, "It's not the adversity that you face but how you face the adversity that builds character and defines you as a person. Now let's win the play-off."

With a par on the first play-off hole, I became the first and only African American to win the San Diego City Women's Amateur Championship.

I learned a valuable lesson that day and reaffirmed what I already knew: Golf provides an opportunity to develop mental toughness and builds character. It requires self-discipline, it teaches you perseverance, integrity, and courtesy, and because it is an individual game, when on the golf course, you learn to depend on your wits, make sound decisions, and live and accept the consequences for your actions.

A champion in life has demonstrated, with a little luck and hard work, that the long hours practicing their craft pays off in the winner's circle. If you ask any storekeeper, teacher, parent or CEO, they would all agree that dedication, desire, and determination are pivotal in contributing toward lifelong goals and success.

Success does not come cheap. There are many personal sacrifices to be made, and a strong support system is critical, and undoubting faith in one's ability helps to build character, the strength of character needed to become a champion. I would carry that lesson with me to college. Let's see how it changed my journey.

A successful junior golf career is no guarantee of a successful college or professional golf career. Despite my junior golf track record and winning the California PGA Junior Championship in 1979, United States International University (USIU) was the only Division I school that offered a full scholarship.

The golf coach Ms. Laura Day, LPGA, was building a very strong and competitive program, and attending USIU was one of the best decisions I ever made.

Here are just a few of the highlights.

- 1982-1983 Rookie of the year U.S.I.U.
- As a four-year letterman, USIU qualified for the NCAA Women's Golf Championship each year.
- I won the first National Minority Collegiate Golf Tournament.
- In 1984, my stroke average was 75.23, and I was ranked twenty-fifth among NCAA Division I golfers nationwide.
- I won medalist honors in tournament events with schools like USC, UCLA, Stanford, San Diego State, and Arizona in the field.
- I had an opportunity to play with teammates from South Africa, Belgium, Sweden, and Colombia.
- I earned a degree in communications.

In addition to a flourishing golf game and valuable life experiences, I was able to use the other interpersonal skills inherent to golf in succeeding in college: learning to be responsible, developing self-confidence, learning good time management skills, and applying these skills during your everyday life, as well as learning how to socially interact with people from all lifestyles. Finally and most importantly, for the first time in my life, I really learned about humility.

As a communications major, I frequently ran across interesting articles from various media throughout the United States. To

my surprise on July 29, 1984, I was featured in the *Grit Magazine*, Williamsport, Pennsylvania, with nine hundred thousand readers.

Below is an excerpt:

## College Golfer Overcomes Many Personal Handicaps.

Like most golfers, Avis has worked hard to reduce her handicap. Just three or four strokes off her game will make the 19-year old San Diego native a [scratch] player.

But the scholarship student at United States International University in San Diego, where she will be a junior this fall, has some handicaps of a different nature in working toward a future goal—joining the Ladies Professional Golf Association Tour.

The barriers Brown has overcome already are not related to the statistics against her in her bid for a players' card. If she succeeds, she would become only the third black to ever compete on the women's tour. In recent years no blacks have played the LPGA circuit.

The article was written after the golf season in 1984. The season where my stroke average was 75.23 and I was ranked 25th among NCAA

Division I golfers nationwide. I fully realized that I was just one of many shining stars; one of many who shared the same dream and ambitions. More importantly, the road to the LPGA was going to be tough one. Did I use this as motivation? Let's find out, as I continue the next chapter of my amazing journey.

# Chapter Five

# Chasing My LPGA Dream

As I stated earlier, once you catch the golf fever, golf becomes more than a game; it becomes a way of life, and as far back as I can remember; I often found myself dreaming at night and daydreaming in school about hitting that cutch shot and making a ten-foot putt to win the tournament. I had the game, maturity, mental toughness, the strength of character needed to become a champion, the three Ds (desire, dedication, or determination), and most importantly, a college degree.

The decision to become a professional golfer was a no-brainer.

I had two major problems:

1.   No money!
2.   No car!

In the back of my mind, I kept hearing the words.

*College Golfer Overcomes Many Personal Handicaps.*

"Like most golfers, Avis has worked hard to reduce her handicap. But the scholarship student at United States International University in San Diego, has some handicaps of a different nature in working toward a future goal—joining the Ladies Professional Golf Association Tour. The barriers Brown has overcome already are not related to the statistics against her in her bid for a players' card. If she succeeds, she would become only the third black to ever compete on the women's tour. In recent years no blacks have played the LPGA circuit."

The road to the LPGA was going to be a tough one, and YES, I used the GRIT article as motivation. I was determined not to let my amazing journey end without trying.

One of my mother's favorite sayings is "When one door closes, God will open another."

I remembered how our family doctor had paid for me and my brother Oran to play in the 1st National Minority Collegiate Championship in Cleveland Ohio held at Highland Park in 1986.

So I took a leap of faith and asked Dr. Charlie Johnson if he would sponsor my dream to play on the LPGA. I am a witness of God's Glory and Greatness. Dr. Charlie Johnson not only brought me a car, he also sponsored me for four years.

The time spent traveling the United States, much of the time alone, playing in Mini tour golf events, was indeed an experience that I would not trade for the world. I met amazing people, visited some beautiful places, and tested my golf game on some very challenging courses.

Here are just a few of the highlights.

- I played on the Players West Professional Golf Tour.
- I played on the Group Fore WPGT.
- I played on the official developmental of the LPGA—Futures tour from 1988 to 1992.
- I qualified and earned playing status the Futures Tour in 2006.
- I set the women's course record of seven under par 65 at Canyon Crest Country Club during the Michelob Golf Classic.
- In 1988, I won the Sectional Qualifying for the United States Women's Open.
- In 1988, I played in the United States Women's Open.
- I was blessed with the opportunity to have played in one-hundred-plus professional golf events.

- I won three mini Tour Golf Championships in four years.
- I was a three-time finalist at the LPGA qualifying school.

Not every day was rosy or full of sunshine; I faced many social challenges. I did, at times, just wanted to quit, pack my bags, and go home. My brother Gordon Jr. once shared some of our grandfather's wisdom and knowledge with me, and I quote, "The time changes fast, but the times do not."

Dr. Charlie Johnson once said to me, "Avis, life is like a maze. You start at A and you'll end at Z. Keep navigating yourself. If there is a wall, turn around. If you have to go up or down, left, or right . . . just keep walking." I have carried that saying with me for forty-three years. Thank you, Dr. Charlie Johnson, for your support during my years of playing amateur and professional golf.

Champions are winners at succeeding in life, and everyone's success meter is different: for me, I had the opportunity of a lifetime, and my dream had come true. My professional golf career and life experiences helped me to mature, made me mentally tough. I had shown strength of character and applied the three Ds that would one day save my life. It gives me chills just thinking about it. What an opportunity.

Golf is just a game; you should build your life around golf and not golf around your life. Yes! The road to the LPGA was worth it, and one of the toughest things we face in life is to know when to say when. Let's find out what is in store for the next chapter of my amazing journey.

# Chapter Six

# How Golf Prepared Me for the Business World

After twenty-five years of playing competitive golf, I took my life experiences, organization, and people skills into corporate America. For twenty-three wonderful years, I have enjoyed being a part of the FedEx family, where I currently serve as an Operations Manager.

## *1. The Psychology of It All*

In chapter 1, our conversation included the following: competition is a part of everyday life, and society places tremendous emphasis centered on winning and losing, and boy, is the Business World competitive. I have managed to keep my sanity by focusing on the bigger and more noble target, using my golf building tools. Yes! By understanding the game being methodical in my approach, and mastering the rules allowed me to successfully process the ups and downs of interpersonal and job relationships, career challenges, and obstacles.

As Matt Blair stated, "If you have given your best, pushed yourself as hard as possible and you still don't win, rejoice in your effort. Rejoice." Sometimes you want to celebrate even defeats, especially, when in your heart, you have given your all.

## The End Goal

Again, as stated in chapter 1, the end goal of competition is to accelerate the development of the tools you need to reliably hit the performance sweet spot on any given day. The focus must be on the development of tools that will serve anyone when they are called on to exhibit character and/or leadership throughout their life, not on wins and losses.

Behavior is not innate; it is learned. One of the key behaviors that I learned at an early age and used to help me become a champion in golf, the workplace, and life, and this did not come easy, when faced with a critical situation or event, I incorporated my approach of positive thinking.

Here is a real-life example: I lost a three-stroke lead with three holes to play. That was the bad news. Here was the good news. I was now tied and still had a chance to win. I won the San Diego Women's City Amateur because I focused on the positive.

## 2. Giving Back to the Community

My life experiences have taught me that things do not happen by chance; there is a reason.

Remaining humble, well grounded, and appreciative of the opportunity to compete and test your skills against competition is one of the reasons why Hall of Fame golfer Tom Watson has had major success long into his senior golf career.

More importantly, a true champion builds a legacy by recognizing that they are now empowered to have a measurement of influence, which can significantly influence the lives of others. They learn through life experiences to check their ego at the door, treat people with dignity, respect and give back to others through charity giving, their personal time, or other contributions.

I hate to beat a dead horse, but if you take anything away from this book, remember, I strongly believe that golf is just a game; you should build your life around golf and not golf around your life.

**I also believe in building tomorrow's leaders today!**
**We can accomplish this by**
**"Empowering women and children with**
**knowledge, opportunity, and awareness."**

Golf has always been my passion; it has provided me and my family with wonderful memories. Being blessed with a special talent, my dream for the world is that every child has the opportunity to experience the game of golf.

Let's find out what is in store for the next chapter of my amazing journey.

# Chapter Seven

# My Battle with the Big C

The world is full of people who do exceptional and extraordinary things, overcome traumatic events in their lives, inspiring others by giving back to their communities, and we never hear about them. Many of us don't pay attention or become actively involved with other people's misfortunes unless it impacts us or someone we know and love.

## *1. You Never Think That It Could Happen to You——————*

No one knows the exact causes of breast cancer. Doctors seldom know why one woman develops breast cancer and another doesn't, and most women who have breast cancer will never be able to pinpoint an exact cause. What we do know is that breast cancer is always caused by damage to a cell's DNA.

I was notified by my Primary Care Physician, Dr. Patricia Pisinger, that I had developed breast cancer. Once, I got beyond the shock, understood what I was faced with and my treatment options, I then informed my family and friends. It was not until then that reality had set in. In forty-two years of playing golf, I had played thousands of rounds of golf, and I knew that I was about to play the toughest round of golf of my life.

## 2. The Toughest Eighteen Holes of My Life————

My brother Gordon Brown Jr. once told me, "It is not the adversity that you face, but how you face the adversity that defines you as a person and builds character." Remembering these words, I knew that I had to come up with a game plan to beat the Big C. In the spring of 2010, I began my battle with breast cancer.

We humans have extraordinary defense mechanisms. One such mechanism is our ability to tap into and rely on past experiences. Early on in junior golf career, I began applying a simple concept that would become my hallmark and help to build the foundation for becoming a champion golfer. But now, I knew that I had to rely on my faith in God and prayers for answers.

Once again, God gave me a blessing; He delivered two of the best doctors in La Jolla, California. My primary doctor's name was Dr. Julie Barone, and my oncologist's name was Dr. Jennifer Fisher. The wonders of modern medicine are only as good as those who know how to apply it.

I was diagnosed with the worst type of breast cancer; invasive ductual carsanomia, stage four. I was treated by the maximum amount of chemo in order to save my life, which caused nerve damage known as neuropathy. The pain was horrible, and there is no cure for it. I would like to give a special shout-out to Dr. Ramona Deonauth, California. She was my guardian angel. Her acupuncture treatments helped to save my life and gave me the relief I needed to continue to live.

While my game plan worked for me, and it may or may work for others, but you never know.

1. Have faith in God and go to him in prayer.
2. Complete the chemotherapy treatments.
3. Get plenty of physical activity.
4. Maintain a healthy diet.
5. Limit the amount of daily stress.
6. Create a support system of positive high-energy people.

As soon as I gained my strength, I began a regiment of physical exercises. I believe that it helped to boost my immune system, but it did not help to keep my weight in check.

My diet included a nutritious, low-fat diet (thirty grams or less) with plenty of fruits and green and orange vegetables, both liquid and solid. I also drank water with 90 percent alkaline. During one of my post-cancer follow-up visits with my oncologist, she stated, "Avis, you look amazing, what are you doing?" I informed her of my physical fitness routine and diet.

I also want to thank my dear cousin Theda Grant. She sent me the miracle box: she labeled each container and the total was $500 worth of vitamins, omega chews, fish oil, and cream to get my skin soft. Her peer at work (Raython) in Washington, DC, had cancer, and she always went to work looking so healthy. Well, Theda decided to send me everything that her peer was taking.

My doctors just could not believe how healthy I looked, so I shared the list of items I was eating and drinking with them for the other cancer patients.

The following is nothing more than using common sense. Limit the amount of daily stress. In 2012, some research studies have shown that factors such as traumatic events and losses can alter immune system functions, and when immune functions are altered, cancer cells may have an opportunity to get them established within one's body. What has been shown is that it is not the fact that a major life crisis has occurred but instead how the individual reacted to this event and coped (or didn't cope). Therefore, identifying ways to keep your stress level in check is wise.

During my chemo treatments, another dear friend, Donna Richardson Joyner, was sending me via mail sermons of Bishop T. D. Jakes Sermon. Former NFL Emitt Smith's wife, Patricia, would drop the sermon packets to Donna's house, and she would mail them to me. I would get so excited when I received new CDs. I would lie in bed and listen to gospel music. It comforted my soul. I would also tune in to Bishop T. D. Jakes. He was my saving grace. I strongly recommend some form of daily meditation. I guess it's true when they say a sound mind makes for a sound body.

Donna also took a trip to San Diego; we attended an event and played in a golf tournament. During dinner, she gave me a Body Gospel Packet consisting of nutrition and Donna's exercise CDs. When I had the energy, I would exercise to gospel and her exercise program. It was a blessing.

You have to believe in your heart and soul that you can beat the Big C. Along with my strong faith in God, I created a support system of positive high-energy people. Daily interaction with your support system is key to your mental state of mind.

I was blessed to have a support system of positive high- energy people; my siblings, Rosetta, Horace and Oran were a schedule rotation to take care of me, so that my husband James could continue to work. Super Model Beverly Johnson knew what I was battling and faced with, called weekly to check on me. I had met and played golf with her at the Black Enterprise Pepsi Golf and Tennis Challenge at La Costa Tennis and Golf Resort in San Diego, Ca.

Although my entire family surrounded me with love and support, there were three special events that helped push me over the top in my fight with cancer. In my third month of treatment, my brother Gordon had just started a new job in a new city. Each day for two months, Gordon would rush home and immediately call me. At the end of each call, he would say, "It is not the adversity that you face but how you face the adversity that defines you as a person and builds character."

After my last treatment of chemotherapy, Donna Richardson Joyner called and asked me to come visit her in Dallas, Texas. That was a very enjoyable week. We played golf, visited the spa, went for morning walks, out to dinner, and she took me to her church, and we sat in the front row, and I was so excited because it was Bishop T. D. Jakes's church. I had prayed for that day, so it was a dream comes true. Within five minutes, Bishop T. D. Jakes was standing five feet in front of me. All I kept saying was "Thank you, Jesus." I couldn't stop the tears from falling.

It was very hard for my children to see me go through the toughest eighteen holes in my life. I told them not to be afraid, Mommy was a champion, and champions always win. Ayanna tried to keep herself busy with school, track and cheerleading. She would video tape her events and share them with me. However, my nine- year- old son, Amari, would run home every day to be by my side. That gave me hope that I would do what it took to stay alive for my family..

I had just finished from one of my chemotherapy treatments and had to pick Amari up from school. When he got in the car, he said, "Mommy, are your feeling OK?" I said "Yes, Amari, the chemo has me a little weak." Amari then said, "Mommy, I don't want you to die. You need to be in the stands at my first Major League Baseball game, holding a sign, saying 'Go, Amari.' I need you, Mommy."

It was this event that was the turning point for me, giving me the inspiration, willpower, and incentive to beat the Big C and be there for my son. As I reflect on this moment, I realize just how great God's glory is and that Golf is a metaphor for life.

When my doctor first told me that I had breast cancer, I knew then that God had chosen me as the miracle of life, and I would be reborn again. Today, my body is pure, and my skin is as soft as a baby, and it is very hard to see my true age. God spared my life for a purpose, and this is my story, and my purpose is to share with the world that you must never give up even when someone discourages you, and prepare for road blocks in your path. God will navigate you through your journey called life. Whatever path you choose, remember to ask God to take your hand and allow him to walk that journey with you. He will never steer you wrong.

# Chapter Eight

# What Defines a Champion?

The champion has demonstrated, with a little luck and hard work and the long hours practicing their craft, it will pay off in the winner's circle. If you ask any Olympic Gold Medal winner, they would all agree that dedication, desire, and determination is pivotal in contributing toward lifelong goals and success. Success does not come cheap. There are many personal sacrifices to be made, and a strong support system is critical, and undoubting faith in one's ability helps to build character, the strength of character needed to become a champion.

It's amazing how we have never heard of a champion housewife, champion store clerk, or champion schoolteacher. As far back as we can remember, society has defined a champion as a winner of a sporting event. Whether on a team or individual, the champion has conquered a test of skills, mind, body, and soul and has reached the pinnacle of performance.

Ask any housewife, store clerk, or schoolteacher, they would probably say, "My success meter is different, but I meet the criteria of a champion."

We should all strive to build a covenant where foundational relationships establish future legacy through knowledge, opportunity, and empowerment, which can assist others in reaching their interpersonal achievements, goals, and self-awareness, making them a champion in life.

Through the eyes of a working mother, wife, golf champion, and cancer survivor, I want to share with you that champions are winners at succeeding in life, and everyone's success meter is different, whether in home life, sports, school, or the business world. Every champion has a story of how they reached the top, and this is my story.

## 1. What do Champions Know That We Do Not?————

Here is what champions do that many of us do not: they understand, harness, and apply the principles of dedication, desire, and determination to help achieve success in life.

### The Three Ds

Dedication, desire, and determination are essential key elements in the building of a champion. They are interconnected characteristics that all successful people have in common, and they use these characteristics to achieve greatness in sports, business, education, and immeasurable contributions to society, which benefits all walks of life, i.e., Mary Bethume-Cookman, Warren Buffet, Nancy Lopez, Bill Gates, your first-grade teacher, and the volunteer at the nursing home, to name a few.

### What Is Dedication?

I have always asked myself, How important is it to be dedicated to your goal? Is the level of your dedication an indicator toward the amount of success? And finally, can we truly measure dedication? Webster defines *dedication* as "a devoting or setting aside for a particular purpose; or self-sacrificing devotion and devotion is the art of showing ardent love or affection." I like to think of dedication as the quality of being dedicated or committed to a task or purpose.

Most of us think that in order to be a successful golfer, computer programmer, or schoolteacher, you have to breathe, eat, and live for our profession or hobby, and that profession or hobby is all that matters. If we do not put 100 percent of our time and energy into our craft or sport, then we are not truly dedicated.

We have all seen movies or heard stories where parents push their children so hard it eventually leads to the brink of physical and emotional destruction. Using their parental powers of persuasion, the parent often measures the child's level of dedication by amount of time engaged in the activity or task. Subsequently, the child often becomes disillusioned, rebels, and quits. Without proper intervention to rescue the child's psyche, many fall prey to becoming a dysfunctional adult.

On a personal note: When my nephew was in high school, he was a straight A student, demonstrated the potential to be a very good golfer, and had a passion for the performing arts and theater. He was dedicated and showed devotion to all three arenas. Fortunately, his grandparents not only empowered with the tools, resources, and assets, but displayed support and encouragement for his passions and dreams. Subsequently, he found his niche and received a golf scholarship to a major university. Today he is PGA certified.

I also have a teenager who has the potential to become a great golfer; he has one of the best golf swings I have seen. He too is dedicated to one of his passions, baseball. As a result of gaining shared knowledge from my parents, my husband and I have provided the opportunities and empowered our teen to experience multiple avenues where he can develop, grow, and excel as a person.

Finally, to prove my point, no one can argue that during his peak, the great Jack Nicholas did not demonstrate his dedication to be the best golfer ever, or argue that he was not a devoted family man, or argue that he was not determined to be a successful golf course designer, businessperson, and major contributor to his community. Mr. Nicholas has simply shown, trying to measure dedication is in the eye of the beholder, it is the quality of dedication, and devotion is the art of showing ardent love or affection for your passions and sharing with others.

## *What Is Desire?*

*Desire* is defined as "a sense of longing or hoping for a person, object, or outcome." I also believe that desire is a conscious impulse toward an experience that promises enjoyment or satisfaction in its attainment.

Although the two are interconnected, please do not get desire and dedication confused. While dedication can lead to the showing of ardent love or affection toward your passions and sharing with others, desire is interpersonally related.

Each person's level of self-attainment is different, so we have to ask, can one truly measure desire? For example, let's say that John, a 2-handicap who has been playing golf for twenty-five years, and Jim, a 10-handicap who has been playing golf for three years, are playing in the club championship.

They both have the desire to compete and win the championship. They practice hard, take golf lessons to sharpen their games, and have studied the course for weeks. However, John's interpersonal desire is not only to win but to break the course record, while Jim's interpersonal desire is to be competitive and not embarrass himself by shooting a higher score than his handicap.

On a personal note, it was during the final round of the San Diego Women's City Amateur, where Patty Benedit, who played with me on our high school golf team, and I were in the final group, and both of us had expressed a strong desire to win the San Diego Women's City Amateur. On the last hole, I held a one-stroke lead and made a bogey. Patty made a par, and we were tied. Did that bogey mean that I had less desire to win than Patty? As the football sport announcer Lee Corso likes to say, "Not so fast, my friend." Up to that point, I had won forty-six junior golf tournaments, and my desire to experience the self-filling enjoyment and gratification with each tournament win grew from within.

My life experiences have taught me that things do not happen by chance; there is a reason. Fortunately for me, my brother Gordon Jr. was caddying for me during the tournament, pulled me aside, and gave me one of his famous mentoring talks prior to the play-off.

I remember him saying, "It's not the adversity that you face but how you face the adversity that builds character and defines you as a person."

Subsequently, I won the play-off on the first hole with a par and became the first and only African-American to win the San Diego Women's City Amateur. I guess old Webster was right. Desire is "a conscious impulse toward an object or experience that promises enjoyment or satisfaction in its attainment," because I felt on top of the world when I received the first place trophy.

One of the best gifts my dad gave us was never questioning our desire to excel at anything we faced. I believe that people innately endeavor mentally and physically to attain enjoyment or gratification. Simply, trying to measure desire is in the eye of the beholder. Each person's level of self-attainment is different. Little did I know some thirty years later that the events, life experiences and my brother's words of wisdom during the San Diego Women's City Amateur would help to save my life.

## *What Is Determination?*

*Determination* is defined as a positive emotion that involves persevering toward a difficult goal in spite of obstacles. I also believe that determination is the power or habit of deciding definitely and firmly.

Yes, determination "is a quality which makes you want to continue trying to do or achieve something that is difficult." Like desire and dedication, determination is not quantifiable; either you have it or you do not. During my college years, I played on the same team with LPGA player Helen Alfredsson. It was apparent through her hidden determination that Helen was going to make it and be successful on the LPGA.

So how does the champion use determination to achieve success? A champion must experience the trials and tribulations of failure before they can enjoy the thrills of success. A parent will painfully watch their baby fall down and not help them up, knowing that through trial, error, and determination, the baby will finally master the art of walking.

During the formative years, our teachers and parents actually begin introducing the determination principle for becoming a champion in life. For those who are fifty years and older, think back to your first-grade teacher. Remember the little stars on the board next to your name; you would get a star for not talking in class for a month or getting 100 percent on the spelling test. Today's generation is a lot different. Parents give their first-grader a cell phone for not talking in class for a day.

Based on my life experiences, determination, if channeled properly, can be a powerful tool. Once you have made a firm decision and commitment, it becomes easier to focus on achieving personal goals.

A true champion builds a legacy by recognizing that they are now empowered to have a measurement of influence, which can significantly influence the lives of others. They learn through life experiences to check their ego at the door, treat people with dignity, respect and give back to others through charity, giving their personal time or other contributions.

The virtues of a champion are not defined by the number of times they step up on the podium but by the foundational relationships and number of lives they can have a positive impact on.

A champion is anyone who has learned how to win in life.

Another prime example of a person who took the three Ds and made it work is one of my heroes, Calvin Peete. I had the pleasure of working with Mr. Peete at a golf clinic. For those of you who do not know his story:

Mr. Peete picked golf up late in life. No storybook junior golf or college career experience, he worked on a farm in Ft. Myers, Florida and had an obstacle: his left arm is shorter than his right. Long story short, Calvin Peete applied dedication, desire, and determination to become a multiple tournament winner on the PGA.

So when you have lost the finals in County Fair Cake Contest for the tenth year in a row and the winners keep flashing that blue ribbon in your face, just remember, you have applied the three Ds and are a champion. How many people can endeavor the mental and physical challenge to attain enjoyment or satisfaction in reaching the finals for ten years in a row.

## 2. In Pursuit of Self-Fulfillment and Happiness———

I am a firm believer that *champions* are winners at succeeding in life, and everyone's success meter is different, whether in sports or the business world. Whether a beginner, intermediate, or advance golfer, we can all benefit from the knowledge, opportunity, and empowerment that golf has to offer. It enhances everyday life skills and promotes a readiness level to face and conquer daily challenges and opportunities.

Golf has always been my passion; it has provided me and my

family with wonderful memories. Being blessed with a special talent, my dream for the world is that every child has the opportunity to experience the game of golf.

## 3. Giving Back———

I had the pleasure of serving as a high school golf coach and twenty-four years as a teaching professional for the San Diego Inner City

Junior Golf Foundation. No matter where I am at, work, church, golfing events, and speaking engagements, you will always hear me stating, "What a great feeling, being able to give back to the children in the community."

## 4. The Challenges

In November 2009, I had a vision and dream: to write a series of books, the first being *Building of a Champion*, and traveling the world in the hope of inspiring children by sharing my amazing story. Along with my business partner, Gordon Jr., we began to put the pieces in place. In early 2010, I was diagnosed with breast cancer, and I believe that God had chosen me as the miracle of life, and I would be reborn again. God spared my life for a purpose, and this is my story, and my purpose is to share with the world that you must never give up even when someone discourages you and prepares road blocks in your path. God will navigate you through your journey called life. Whatever path you choose, remember to ask God to take your hand and allow him to walk that journey with you. He will never steer you wrong.

## 5. The Rewards

I am cancer-free, Gordon Jr. and I have assembled a dream team, and along the way, we have met some extraordinary people. Our quest for the Avis Brown-Riley Golf Extravaganza continues. My dream for the world is that every child has the opportunity to experience the game of golf. No matter how long the day has been, I find time on Facebook, watching and analyzing golf swings, providing words of encouragement and advice to my many Facebook friends (youths) from Africa and the United States. There is a need, a hunger, a thirst, and we are on a mission to *promote golf and health awareness, provide opportunities, and empower women and children around the world.*

James Thomas Anthony Valvano, nicknamed Jimmy V, was an American college basketball player, coach, and broadcaster. While the head coach at North Carolina State University, his team won the 1983 national title against improbable odds.

Here are my two favorite Jim Valvano Quotes:

> How do you go from where you are to where you want to be? I think you have to have an enthusiasm for life. You have to have a dream, a goal, and you have to be willing to work for it.
>
> *Jim Valvano*
>
> Don't give up, don't ever give up.
>
> *Jim Valvano*

Coach Jimmy V was right, You have to have a dream, a goal, and you have to be willing to work for it. Don't give up, don't ever give up. On July 17, 2017, tears of joy rolled down my eyes and calmness reigned in my soul. After 25 years, my dream had come true. I received word that I was officially LPGA Certified.

## 6. Building a Champion in Life

A life champion must experience the trials and tribulations of success and failure before they can enjoy the thrills of victory. Not to beat a dead horse, but let's keep it real. We are taught the following from childhood: everyone wants to be a winner and associate with winners. It is a part of the America DNA. Although the time changes, the times do not change; our society is not structured for building champions in life.

A true champion builds a legacy by recognizing that they are now empowered to have a measurement of influence, which can significantly influence the lives of others. They learn through life experiences to check their ego at the door, treat people with dignity, respect, and give back to others through charity, giving their personal time or other contributions.

The virtues of a champion are not defined by the number of times they step up on the podium but by the foundational relationships and number of lives they can have a positive impact on.

I would like to thank golf legends Al Duhon and Bill Wright for helping to pave the way.

Bill Wright, Avis, and Gordon Brown, Sr.   Al Duhon, Avis, and Gordon Brown, Sr.

A Christian woman, wife, working mother, and soon-to-be businesswoman, Avis's coworkers, managers, family, and friends define her as a person who is dependable, trustworthy, of strong moral character, and a great team player.

As a Cancer survivor and professional golf instructor, I am a firm believer that champions are winners at succeeding in life, and everyone's success meter is different, whether in sports or the business world. Whether a beginner, intermediate, or advance golfer, we can all benefit from the knowledge, opportunity, and empowerment that golf has to offer. It enhances everyday

54

life skills and promotes a readiness level to face and conquer daily challenges and opportunities.

By the grace of God! I am cancer-free. It was a long, hard fight, and I believe the Lord spared me so that I can share my walk of life and help to inspire others through health awareness and golf.

Here is my testimony: I had played golf for thirty-five years, and after I stopped playing regularly, my joints began to get hard, leaving me with restricted flexibility, bending and turning motion. In 2009, I met Dr. William Wilson, who specializes in pain management. For the past eight years, I had experienced lower back problems with my L4 and L5 joints.

Dr. Wilson treated my L4 and L5 joints by performing a lateral branch block. It relieved the pain and gave me flexibility for approximately two years. Dr. Wilson recommended radio frequency—burning the nerves to both joints on both sides. It is a very delicate and painful procedure, but I knew that I was in good hands with Dr. Wilson, one of the best pain management doctors in San Diego. My most recent radio frequency back surgery was performed by Dr. Wilson on January 5, 2017. It will give me relief for approximately two years. This allows me to play golf and enjoy my passion.

I believe that one of the greatest gifts a person can give to another is the sharing of life experiences. As our forefathers have proven, through this gift, we help to build character, hope, and a road map for self-defined success.

Golf has always been my passion. It has provided me and my family with wonderful memories. Being blessed with a special talent, my dream for the world is that every child has the opportunity to experience the game of golf.

# Chapter Nine

# Golf History Chronology

I am blessed, and golf has provided me with opportunities beyond my wildest dreams. Here are just a few of my golf career highlights:

| Year | Accomplishments |
|---|---|
| 1973 | Won first Junior Golf Tournament |
| 1974 | Won Junior World Championship |
| 1975–1982 | Placed in the Junior World Championship (3 times) |
| 1974–1982 | Won 46 San Diego Junior Golf Association Tournaments |
| 1974–1982 | Won the San Diego Junior Golfer of the Year (5 times) |
| 1979 | Girls' Junior America's Cup – Team Matches, 1st Place |
| 1979 | Junior Team Championship - 2nd Place Team at Ranch Bernardo Inn |
| 1981 | Won the Southern California Junior PGA Championship |
| 1982-1983 | Rookie of the year U.S.I.U |
| 1984 | Won San Diego Women's City Amateur Champion |
| 1984 | Inducted into the San Diego Golf Hall of Fame |
| 1986 | Won the First National Minority Collegiate Golf Championship |
| 1988–1992 | Over 100 Professional Golf events |
| 1988–1992 | Played on the LPGA Futures Tour |

| 1988 | US Women's Open participant |
|------|------|
| 1988–2016 | San Diego Inner City Junior Golf Foundation—Teaching Professional |
| 1997 | Inducted into the African American Golfers Hall of Fame |
| 2004 | High School Golf Coach |
| 2006 | Qualified to play on the LPGA Futures Tour |
| 2015 | Passed Stage 1 of the LPGA Certification program |
| 2017 | LPGA Certification - Apprentice |

I was inducted into the San Diego Hall of Champions and the African American Golfers Hall of Fame, where I serve as a board member.

# How I Became a Champion in Life: The Avis Brown-Riley Story

*It is not the adversity that you face but how you face the adversity that defines you as a person and builds character.*

Avis will donate some of the book proceeds to the following Non-Profit Organizations: San Diego Inner City Junior Golf Foundation.

"I think what Avis Brown and her family have done throughout their careers in the golf world is nothing short of amazing. Avis is a wonderful player and teacher and readily offers her experience to helping others learn this game. That passion is so important to the growth of golf, and we need more golf professionals like her going into the future."

Byron Casper
International PGA (lifetime member),
Son of Hall of Fame Golf Legend Billy Casper

"An extraordinary journey by an ordinary person. It will bring tears to eyes and laughter to your soul."

Our society places tremendous emphasis on winning and losing, so much so that we often forget to celebrate the valuable life experiences that are gained.

In the pages of this fascinating journey, Avis shares her trademark three Ds (dedication, desire, and determination) that empowered her to become a golf champion. Little did she know that the lessons learned would one day save her life and help to reach the interpersonal rewards that life has to offer.

Avis is also a mom, who has one daughter, Ayanna, and one son, Amari. She has been married to her husband, James, for twenty-one years. Avis comes from the famous Gordon and Harriet Brown golfing family. She has three brothers and one sister, whose youngest son is PGA certified.

Avis was introduced to the game of golf at age seven. By the age of ten, she became the first African American to win the prestigious Junior World Golf Championship. As a member of the San Diego Junior Golf Association, she won over forty-six golf tournaments and represented San Diego in team events. During her final year of junior golf, she amazingly won ten of sixteen events, finished second twice, and third three times. She won the San Diego Junior Golf Association Junior Golfer of the Year five times.

In 1982, Avis became the first and only African American to win the San Diego City Women's Amateur Championship. Avis attended the United States International University, a Division I college on a golf scholarship. She won the first National Minority Collegiate Golf tournament. In 1984, she was ranked twenty-fifth in the nation, and played in the NCAA Women's Championship every year. She received her degree in communications.

After college, Avis traveled the United States, much of the time alone, playing in mini tour golf events. Her professional golf career is highlighted in 1988, when she shot a seven under par 65 (a women course record) to win the Michelob Classic at Canyon Crest Country

Club. She also played in the United States Women's Open at the Funny Farm Country Club in Baltimore, Maryland.

Avis was inducted into the San Diego Golf Hall of Fame and the African American Golfers Hall of Fame.

Avis credits her strong faith in God, her parents' values of desire, dedication, and determination to become a winner in life, along with her life experiences, as the key factors toward beating her battle with breast cancer. Avis strongly believes that it is not the adversity that you face but how you face the adversity that defines you as a person and builds character.

As her amazing journey continues, Avis looks forward to traveling the world, hosting the Avis Brown-Riley Golf Extravaganza, designed to empower youth and women to reach their goals and becoming a winner in life. No matter where she is at, work, church, golfing events, or speaking engagements, you will always hear Avis say with a sparkle in her eyes, "What a great feeling, being able to give back to the children in the community."

Avis will donate some of the book proceeds to the following Non-Profit Organizations: San Diego Inner City Junior Golf Foundation. The Avis Brown-Riley Golf Extravaganza team has affectionately nicknamed her the Little Warrior.

In July 2017, Avis officially became LPGA Certified. Stay tuned to the next chapter in this amazing journey.